No portion of this book, either artwork, design or text may be reproduced in any form without written permission from Kari Denker, except for brief quotations used in reviews. All rights reserved.

Unless otherwise noted, all Scripture quotations are from The Holy Bible, New American Standard Version, copyright © 1960, 1962, 1963, 1968, 1973, 1975, 1977 The Lockman Foundation.

ESV Study Bible, copyright © 2001, 2008 by Crossway.

All rights reserved. This book or any portion thereof may not be reproduced or used in any manner whatsoever without the express written permission of the author except for the use of brief quotations in a book review.

**To order additional copies of this study,
visit www.StoneSoupforFive.com or Amazon.com.**

Editor: Kristen He
Illustrator: Kristen He
Cover design: Matthew Puckett

Printed in the United States of America

First Printing, 2017

how this Bible study guide works

This study is designed to be used in a way that works into your life. You won't find any homework assignments or fill in the blanks, but rather questions to ponder, items to list and research, suggestions for doodles, and lots of opportunities to add creativity and fun in your own journal.

Research has shown that doodling helps people retain what they are learning, so take advantage of that and doodle as much as possible! I've included lots of examples to get you started. Add those, and experiment with more! Let this guide be a jumping off place for your own experimentation and creativity!

This study can be used in two different ways, you can work through it from first page to last and dig into each theme through all five chapters of the book.

— or —

You can work through it chapter by chapter by starting with chapter one in truth, then flip to chapter one in love, and finally to chapter one in obedience. Then you can work through chapter two in the same way, repeating until you get through all five chapters! I'm all about options!

Mainly, I want you to enjoy your time in God's word, using doodles, lists, and other fun ways to make it easy to remember and apply.

supplies needed

To get the most out of this study (and have a blast doing it), gather these supplies to keep on hand.

- Bible (This study was written mainly with the ESV translation.)

- Composition style notebook or journal. (I don't typically like to go smaller than a composition notebook because I like to be sure I have all the room I need to write and doodle!)

- Markers or colored pencils in green, pink, and blue OR you could gather some washi-style tape with these colors to use instead or in addition to the markers.

- Pen, pencil, and eraser

- optional items are gel pens, stickers, and stamps make it fun too!

introduction

Welcome to our study through 1 John! I'm so excited to have you here. This study is the result of months and months of work because after writing the study through the Gospel of John I thought it would be great to work through his epistle next. Simple enough, right? But, after jumping into this beautiful book I quickly realized that reading it is much different than writing a Bible study guide through it. It is written in a very circular pattern. John has main themes he wrote about, then he circled back around and touched on them again in a slightly different way. The ESV Study Bible calls it a "symphonic" style of writing, comparing it to classical music which has a main theme and then variations on that theme.

In my linear thinking brain it was less classical and more chaotic. It was a struggle to pull out what I could use to make a study deep, meaningful, and life impacting Bible study. I kept getting bogged down with the dizzying pace John moved through his themes and circled back around. It was extremely frustrating, to say the least. After lots of prayer and giving up numerous times in the process, God kept bringing 1 John back to me. This book was truly what I needed to be working on, because the truth in this book truly took my breath away when I was able to pull it out and process it. He knows exactly what we need, despite our most spectacular fits to the contrary. Amen?

So to avoid you having the same frustration, I've written this study different than all my other studies. In this guide, we'll go through each theme in 1 John one at a time, working through all the chapters tracing that theme, then coming back and working through the next theme. This was the key to unlocking it for me. I pray it is for you too.

Now, after finishing the study, I am so thankful the Lord lead me through it and put up with my attitude and countless times of quitting. (Really, I gave up writing this study more times than I can count! Good friends and lots of prayer are the only reasons why you have it in your hands today.) 1 John is a truly remarkable book of assurance, truth, love, and obedience and it was exactly what I needed to hear and learn at the time. As the ESV Study Bible put it, "this is not a list of dos and don'ts. It is a manifesto of 'Done!' First John highlights what God the Father has 'done' in sending Christ the Son, offering Him up as a sacrifice for sins, and sending forth the 'word of life' (1 John 1:1)…"

context

Context is absolutely crucial for any good Bible study. You might be tempted to skip this step but I encourage you to make this the most important first step of your time in working through 1 John.

- ☐ At the top of your first journal page, draw a music staff and notes to remind you of the symphonic (or circular or spiral) style of writing. Under that, write the main theme for 1 John (assurance) and the three sub themes we'll be studying (truth, love, and obedience). Have fun with looking up some fun fonts to write those in. Lisa, over at www.creativelei.com has some great tips for lettering that you might want to check out too.

- ☐ If your Bible has an introduction of 1 John, read that and underline or take notes of anything that stands out to you. If your Bible doesn't have one, there are many great ones online through Blue Letter Bible or Grace to You (gty.org).

- ☐ Because the history points to this epistle being written toward the end of John's life, while he was in Ephesus, draw a simple map of the region. (I've drawn one on the next page that you can trace or copy from if you'd like.)

- ☐ For your final part of digging into the context check out **The Bible Project** on YouTube and search for 1-3 John. They have a great overview of the book in a fun doodle style that I LOVE. (Plus, they're Portland based, so I love them even more!) https://www.youtube.com/watch?v=l3QkE6nKylM

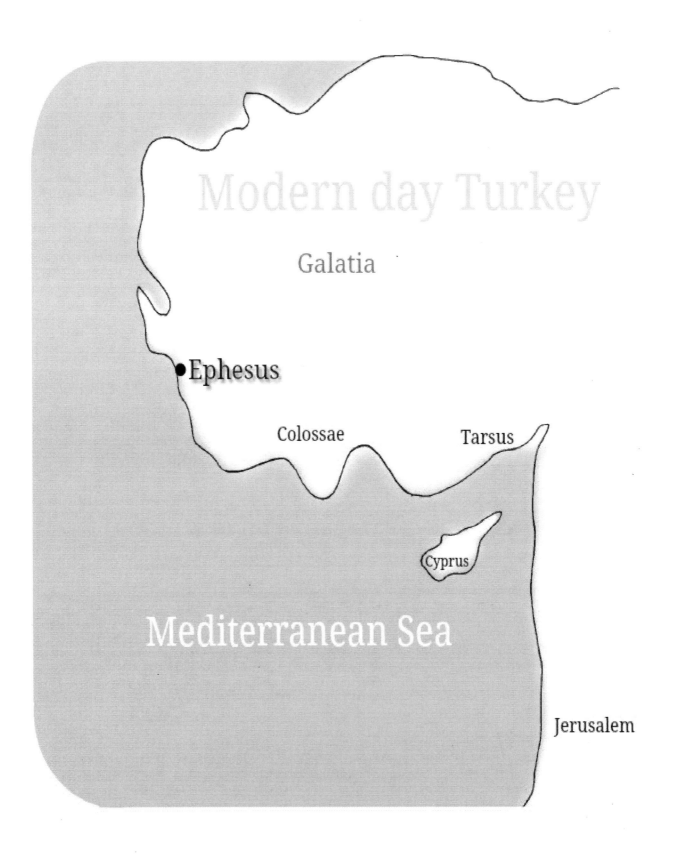

map

overview

☐ First let's get a good overview of the book of 1 John. Flip through your Bible and write each chapter heading and subheading of all chapters in your journal.

☐ Read through the entire book of 1 John. If you're short on time break it up by reading just one chapter at a time. It takes about 15 to 20 minutes to read through. Check off each chapter as you read it.

- ☐ chapter 1
- ☐ chapter 2
- ☐ chapter 3
- ☐ chapter 4
- ☐ chapter 5

☐ After reading through the book, do you have any questions about anything you noticed? Write out any questions you have in your journal.

☐ Do you already know some verses from 1 John? Any favorites you've memorized or heard before? Write those down on your journal page too.

☐ The key verse for the book is 1 John 5:13. Write it out and doodle a key next to it.

The epistle of 1 John is rich in doctrine, ethics, and devotion to Christ. John is calling us to grow in the knowledge of truth, love for God and others, and obedience. In other words, he wants us to truly know God, to love God and others, and have our actions be more and more Christ-like.

It is extremely important to remember that the whole purpose of this epistle is ASSURANCE for the believer. Assurance, not condemnation. If you are truly a believer this epistle will encourage and challenge you as you grow more and more like Christ. If you have not accepted Christ's gift of salvation, this epistle will impart to you the importance of what Christ has done on your behalf.

Who was John?

☐ John never mentions his name in this epistle (or in his gospel), but these three books are credited to the disciple John, an apostle of Jesus and a leader in the early church. It is believed he is the same apostle who wrote John and Revelation. (The similarities between John and 1 John are striking!) From early in church history, this epistle was unquestionably accepted as John's letter and the historical evidence backs this up. This study won't get into the history of the authorship, but if you love digging deep I encourage you to add your own research on the background into your journal.

☐ On your journal page, draw the apostle John. Next to your doodle of John, write out any of these interesting facts that stand out to you:

- John was the son of Zebedee, a Galilean fisherman, and James' brother (another disciple of Jesus).

- Jesus nicknamed these two brothers the "Sons of Thunder." (Mark 3:17) They were outspoken, bold, and intense. In fact, in Luke 9:51-55 we get a taste of that intensity when they asked Jesus if He wanted them to call down fire from heaven onto his critics.

- John, together with his brother and Peter, were in Jesus' most inner circle of friendship. They alone were with Jesus on the Mount of Transfiguration (Matthew 17) and they alone watched Jesus resurrect Jarius's daughter (Mark 5:37).

- John, whose life was dramatically transformed by his time with Jesus, referred to himself as "the disciple whom Jesus loved" (John 21:20-24).

- In 1 John 3:19-20 we see that John was a loving pastor who knew believers are easily distracted and need repetition. He knew the inward struggle we all have with sin, love, and growing in Christ-likeness. And he knew that God, through His word and His Spirit, reassures our hearts and frees us from condemnation. What a tremendous promise!

☐ Have more time? Read more about John in the following passages: Luke 9:49-50, Mark 10:35-41, Mark 14:32-42, Luke 22:7-13, John 19:25-27, Acts 3:1-11, Acts 4:1-23, Acts 8:14-17, Galatians 2:9.

- [ ] Again, I want to stress this study guide and this epistle are not a list of "to dos" or "to don'ts." Until we grasp the meaning of Christ's completed work on the cross, we will always be tempted to gain God's approval through our own good deeds. Salvation is not about changing a bad person to a good person. It's about a dead person coming to life. And only God can bring what was dead to life. DEAD to LIVING, not bad to good. It's all done through Christ, who conquered sin and death. It was DONE at the cross.

    The very essence of the gospel is that God, in His immense love, sent His Son to die for people who could not help themselves. When we accept this work as payment for our own sins, we are born again, raised to a new life in Christ.

    John tells us that God's grace doesn't stop there, however. God saved us, not only to free us *from* sin, but to free us *to* holiness. That is what 1 John is about: assurance, freedom from sin, responding to God in obedience, and growing in love for Him and others.

- [ ] Spend some time today meditating on these truths of the gospel. Some great verses to start with are: Romans 3:23-25; Colossians 1:13-14; Colossians 1:21-23; Ephesians 1:3-10; Ephesians 2:1-10; 2 Timothy 1:8-10; 1 Peter 1:3-5.

- [ ] After taking notes on those verses, journal about where you think you are right now in your knowledge of the truth, your love for God, your obedience to Christ, and your assurance of salvation.

- [ ] Before you finish today, take time to pour your heart out to God. Tell Him where you are right now and where you'd like to be. He is rich in mercy, full of grace and love.

Now are you ready? Let's do this!

"By this we shall know that we are of the **truth** and reassure our heart before Him..."

truth - 1 John 1

- ☐ Take a moment before we dive in to pray for the Spirit to lead you and give you understanding.

- ☐ Begin by reading 1 John 1

- ☐ Turn to a fresh journal page and write the overall theme of 1 John (assurance) big and bold across the top of the page.

- ☐ Now to the side of that, in the upper corner closest to the edge of the page, write TRUTH. Then take a green marker or colored pencil (or green washi tape) and color or tape down the outer edge of your journal page. You can either do this for every page that we'll mark truths on, or you can simplify and just do it on the first page of the section. We'll do the same with the pink for the love sections and the blue for the obedience sections. This will make it easy for you to see what each section of your study was about.

- ☐ Roughly divide your page in half, either with a light pencil or mentally. On the top of that line, in the center of the page, draw Jesus.

- ☐ On one side of Jesus, write bullet points of what John says about Him in verses 1 and 2 of 1 John.

- ☐ On the other side, write out what the same apostle said about Him in John 1:1-5.

- ☐ Note any similarities with a star or highlight.

truth - 1 John 1

☐ One of the words that appears throughout John's epistle is the Greek word *phaneroo*. It is translated either as "made manifest" or "appeared." On your page, draw a banner and write out either the Greek or English word inside it.

☐ Look up the other verses in 1 John that have this word and write them out under your banner:

    ☐ 1 John 1:2

    ☐ 2:28

    ☐ 3:2,5,8

    ☐ 4:9

☐ Now, look at 3:8 again and write out why Jesus was made manifest. The Greek word *phaneroo* means open to sight, visible, and showing one's true character. Jesus being made manifest was so important to John (and us) because He physically came to earth and lived a holy life showing us who He really is. God in flesh. Why should this matter to you? Journal your thoughts.

☐ John says the reason why the Son of God appeared was to destroy the works of the devil. Why was this truth so important to John? Why should it matter to us today? Write out your thoughts. (Also look up 2 Timothy 1:10, and Hebrews 2:14 and write out or take notes on them to add to your journal page.)

☐ Do these truths about Christ assure you? How? Write your thoughts out in your journal.

truth – 1 John 1

- ☐ On a new page, prep your page with ASSURANCE written across the top and tape or color the side of the page green, with TRUTH written out on the top corner of the page.

- ☐ Re-read chapter 1.

- ☐ Draw a scroll and quill and next to it answer why John wrote this epistle (verse 4). Write it nice and big or in a fun font. Remember the main theme is assurance. How does this reason for writing support that theme?

- ☐ Look up John 15:11 and 16:22. John sounds just like His Savior! The more truth we know and the more we obey it, the more we'll become like Christ. Does this give you joy? Hope? Why? Journal your thoughts.

- ☐ Draw an open Bible in your journal. On it, write out TRUTH. Now work through the following questions in your journal as specifically as possible.

    - What does dedication to studying the Word of Truth look like?
    - How dedicated am I to studying the truth?
    - Can I improve my time spent with God? How?
    - How is my day different when I do read the Bible?
    - What tends to happen when I don't?

- ☐ Be sure that your study of truth is mostly through reading the Word of Truth, but don't neglect what the Holy Spirit has taught others too. Reading good books and listening to sermons and podcasts increase your understanding of the truth too.

- ☐ Take some time today to review your usual weekdays. When and where can you cut something out to make time to improve or increase your time spent with God? Make a decision for this week and write it down even if it is just 10 or 15 minutes and work hard to develop it into a habit.

truth - 1 John 2

☐ On a new page, title the top with ASSURANCE and tape or color the side of the page green, with TRUTH written out on the top outer corner of the page.

☐ Read chapter 2.

☐ Right at the start we have two big, full words. Write out both "advocate" and "propitiation" and then look up and write out the definition for each. Doodle a box or scroll around each.

☐ Notice that it's not "if anyone confesses," but **if anyone sins**. Jesus, the righteous propitiation for our sins, is our Advocate **AS. SOON. AS. WE. SIN.** He isn't angry or brooding or waiting for us to repent before He comes to the Father. He is there before the throne as our Advocate <u>as soon as we sin</u>. Write out what you think about Jesus as YOUR advocate under your definition.

☐ So what is He doing when He stands before the Father? He isn't asking for the Father to forgive us with a heavy sigh and shrug of His shoulders. He's our Propitiation. He's asking the Father for justice because of our sins, because God IS just. And that justice has already been paid—*by Him*. He is both the Just and the Justifier (Romans 3:26). Advocate and Propitiation. He is before the throne saying "Her sin? That's on Me, Father. I've died and paid for this." This truth continues to amaze me. What love! What justice! Journal your thoughts of Jesus as YOUR propitiation under the definition.

☐ Next, look up and write out these verses:

- Romans 8:1
- Romans 8:34
- 1 Timothy 2:5-6
- Hebrews 7:25-27

☐ Do these verses add any insight to Jesus as your advocate and propitiation?

☐ How do these truths give you assurance?

☐ Spend some time praying through these truths.

"I am not what I ought to be,
I am not what I want to be,
I am not what I hope to be in another world;
but still I am not what I once used to be,
and by the grace of God I am what I am."

-John Newton

truth - 1 John 2

- ☐ On a new page, title the top with ASSURANCE and tape or color the side of the page green, with TRUTH written out on the top outer corner of the page.

- ☐ Re-read chapter 2 and draw and ink pot and a quill and write out 1 John 2:1.

- ☐ What are "these things" John is writing to us? They are all of the things he has written so far in his epistle. Glance back over your previous notes and summarize them on this journal page.

- ☐ Write out the second half of verse 8, starting with "because the darkness is passing away…" Draw a dark storm cloud with the sun peeking out and some yellow sunbeams spreading across your page.

- ☐ In the sunbeam area write out verse 12-14, or just the key points. John is re-stating why he is writing. These are powerful truths. If John is repeating them in his book, we would do well to repeat them in our journals, right?

- ☐ Many Bible commentators think that when John is addressing "little children, fathers, and young men" he is speaking to the spiritual status of believers (new, mature, and growing). However, some also think "little children" could be a general reference to all believers and "fathers and young men" could refer to those older and younger. Either way, this section is full of great truths that we need to know! Go back through the truths you wrote out and bold or highlight those that are especially meaningful to you today.

- ☐ What do these truths teach you about God? About yourself?

truth - 1 John 2

- [ ] In verses 15-22 we're introduced to a word only John uses: antichrist (1 John 2:18, 22, 4:3). Note that anti- in Greek can mean both "against" and "instead of."

- [ ] In your journal, write out "antichrist" in big, bold letters. Under that, substitute both definitions of "anti" from above and write them out.

- [ ] So in this section John isn't necessarily speaking of The Antichrist, but of other people who are against Christ, or teach of something instead of Christ. (I might add they could teach of something in addition to Christ, also.) What are some modern day examples of antichrists based on these definitions? What do they teach? How is what they teach contrary to Scripture? Can you refute their teaching with Scripture?

- [ ] Carefully re-read this section and write out any truth you find about antichrists.

- [ ] In this section John also warns us that we (and they) are living in the "last hour" or "last time." In your journal draw an hour glass and write out verse 18 near it.

- [ ] John says, WE KNOW it's the last hour. Understanding that there is quite a time gap between John's time of writing this epistle and our modern time, what do you think "the last hour" means? Write your thoughts in your journal.

- [ ] Bible commentator and pastor Warren Wiersbe puts it this way: *"God is not limited by time the way His creatures are. God works in human time, but He is above time. (2 Peter 3:8) ...The last hour describes a kind of time, not a duration of time. 'The latter times' are described in 1 Timothy 4. Paul, like John, observed characteristics of his time, and we see the same characteristics today in even greater intensity."*

- [ ] John states that you have the Holy One, you have all knowledge (2:20), and have no need that anyone should teach you (2:27). Look up John 14:15-17 and compare these verses. He is saying that what we have heard from the beginning (the simple truth of the Gospel) should be what we're abiding in. But what is the gospel? Take a few minutes to write out what you know of the gospel in your journal. (If you're not sure, look back at page 9 of this study for a starting place.) Another simple way to clarify your thoughts on the gospel is to answer these prompts: I was; Christ did; I am; Christ is; why.

pause and reflect

These first few pages of truth are so deep and rich!

Made manifest

Light

Advocate

Propitiation

Freedom from sin

- ☐ Take some time today and write out a prayer to God based on these truths. Write it on the next blank journal page, or on a separate piece of paper and tape it in your journal.

- ☐ If you're new to praying through Scripture, a good format is to first thank God for anything that stands out to you in the verses.

- ☐ Then pray simple statements to God based on those Scriptures. Statements are always so good for solidifying the truth in our minds and filling our minds with gospel truths.

- ☐ After that, ask some questions. Not "Why God?!" questions, but deep, soul-searching questions such as "Why do I struggle to believe this?" Or "How can I apply this truth to my life in a practical way today?"

- ☐ Then finish up by asking God to help you remember and apply these truths to your life.

We know

"You notice how the apostle constantly writes about knowing. Take your pencil, and underline the word "know" in John's Epistles, and you will be surprised to find how frequently he uses it. He is not one of those who suppose, or fancy, or imagine, or have formed a certain hypothesis; but he knows, and he tells us what he knows, in order that we also may know." -C.H. Spurgeon

- One of the key phrases in 1 John is "we know" or "you know."
- Look up and write out the definition of "know" in your journal.
- List all the "we knows" and "you knows" from this chapter in your journal. (Verses 3, 5, 14, 18, 21, 29.)
- Draw a box around or highlight the "we know" you are most moved or surprised by. Next to it write out your thoughts. Here are some questions to get you started:
  - Why does it impact you?
  - What does it mean to you?
  - What does it teach you about God?
  - How should it change you?
- Leave the rest of the page blank and add to it as you see more "we know" statements.

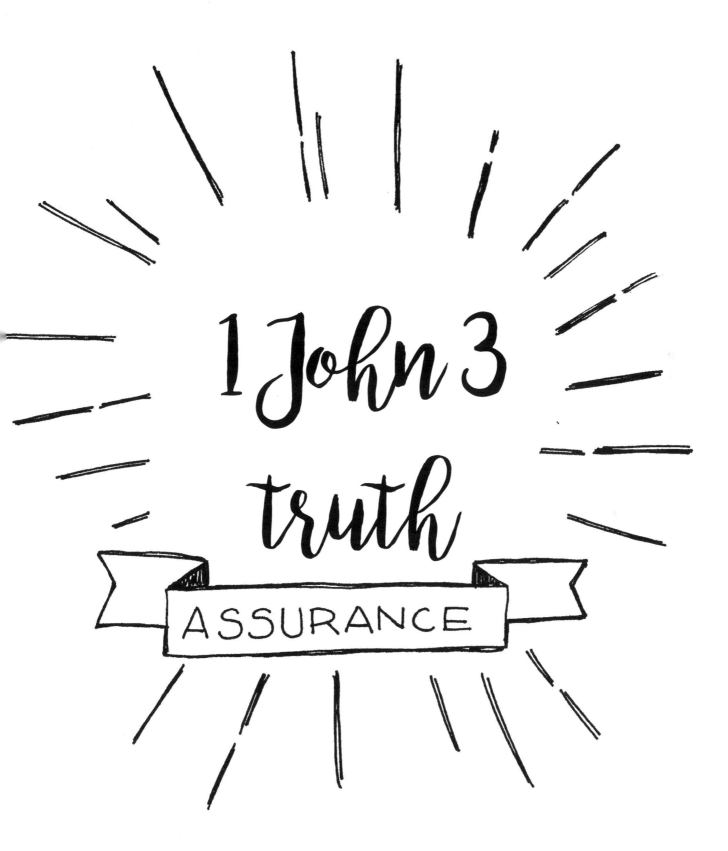

truth - 1 John 3

- ☐ Label a new page with ASSURANCE and TRUTH.

- ☐ Read through chapter 3.

- ☐ In most modern translations verse 1 starts with "see," but I like the King James Version better, as it starts with "Behold!" Write out "behold" big and bold in your journal then write out the verse. (I encourage you to use the King James Version for this one.) The Greek word for behold is so much more than see. It means to be amazed by, to understand, to discern, to inspect, experience, to perceive and to be skilled in. I love that last definition especially, to be skilled in. Rewrite the sentence but substitute one (or all! Extra Credit!) of the definitions for the word "see."

- ☐ Does this truth give you any new thoughts about God? Does it give you any new insight into what you should be doing in light of this love?

- ☐ At the end of verse 1 John states that we are CALLED children of God and we ARE children of God. Our position in God is not just by name, but by position. We are His children. Loved, adopted, born anew. This is one of the greatest wonders of the world. Forget the hanging gardens or pyramids, the fact that me, a sinner, who had her heart set against God was chosen, loved, adopted, and wrapped in His love is a marvel and wonder! In your journal, write your thoughts out to God. Thank Him for all of this wonder and grace.

- ☐ Here in chapter three, we also find an excellent definition of sin. Write out the end of verse 4. Some versions say "sin is breaking the law," or "transgression of the law," but I love the ESV and NASB translation of "lawlessness." A lawless person lives a reckless, uncaring, bold, "I'll do it my way" kind of life. That is what we were. In your journal, write out your own thoughts about what a lawless life looks like today. Think of any examples or stories you've heard and jot a few notes.

- ☐ Now, look back at that beautiful word "behold." We were lawless. We were deliberately against God... but BEHOLD the kind of love that Father has given us! How can you keep this knowledge of God's love constant and alive in your mind and life?

truth – 1 John 3

Verses 11-15 speak to a sensitive issue that Jesus touched on during His sermon on the mount (Matthew 5:22). It's an issue that affects millions of people around the world today in the form of abortion. Here me out… if you have had an abortion, please keep reading… I appreciate what Warren Wiersbe said about these verses: *"The issue here is not whether a murderer can become a Christian, but whether a man can continue being a murderer and still be a Christian. The answer is no."*

There are many people in the Bible who murdered and God in His grace forgave… Moses, David, and Paul are three prominent ones. But someone who lives a lifestyle of hatred and murder cannot also be a true believer. God forgives all who come to Him with a repentant and believing heart. Nothing is too bad or too big for God to forgive or He wouldn't be God and Christ would have died for no reason. God knows what you've been through. He knew before He formed you exactly what your life would be. None of us are worthy of His forgiveness and love, but because He chose us before the beginning of time (2 Timothy 1:9-10), we have been blessed to receive His mercy and grace, and nothing we can or have done will ever remove that from us. Rest in this blessed assurance. It is not about you. It's all about Him.

☐ For those of us who haven't been touched by abortion, use this reminder to pray for those who have. Pray for forgiveness and truth to reach the deep places of their heart and for God's love and forgiveness to penetrate deeply.

☐ Draw a big heart on your page and in it write out 3:20. (It usually works better if you write the verse first, then draw the heart around it, so you don't run out of room.) Our heart is deceitful. It's listed as a fact. Look up and write out Jeremiah 17:9 and Mark 7:21. What does this teach you about yourself?

The Holy Spirit convicts, but our deceitful heart condemns. Conviction leads to repentance, condemnation leads to more condemnation. Assure yourself of this: If you are feeling conviction from the Holy Spirit, it is usually specific—pointing out a specific sinful act or attitude. If you are feeling accusing condemnation it is usually vague, unclear, and general. Let's make a promise to always put more faith in God and less in our feelings and doubts, because God is always and will forever be greater than our heart.

truth – 1 John 4

- ☐ Set up a new page, by titling the top with ASSURANCE and write TRUTH on the top.

- ☐ Read through chapter 4.

- ☐ Divide your page up with a light pencil into thirds. In the top third, draw a stop sign or a yield sign. (This would be pretty cool looking if you drew a big stop sign that partly hung off the edge of the page. Sometimes breaking up the monotony really makes it stand out.)

- ☐ John varies from his usual themes at the start of this chapter to share a warning that we are to test the spirits—spirits that are from false teachers. It goes back to what we read at the end of chapter two about knowing what we believe. He's calling us to be discerning—to be a Berean (Acts 17:11). Next to your stop or yield sign write out verse 1 and/or this quote from Puritan pastor Richard Baxter:

"Read and meditate on the Holy Scriptures much in private. Then you will be the better able to understand what is preached on it in public, and to try the doctrine, whether it be of God. If you are unacquainted with the Scriptures, all that is treated of or alleged from them, will be so strange to you, that you will be but little edified by it."

- ☐ John has been telling us what we are to believe about Christ. But we are not supposed to believe everything we hear about Christ outside of the Bible. We are to be students of the TRUTH. If we study the Word and the person and work of Jesus Christ, the false religions will be obvious. Prepare yourselves to give an answer to those who are taken in by false religions, but study and get to deeply know the Bible.

If there is any question raised about the Deity and the humanity of Christ, do not listen any longer. When you taste the first morsel of meat from a joint, and you find that it is tainted, there is no necessity for you to eat all the rest to see if it is good; and if any man questions the true Divinity and the real humanity of Christ, have nothing to do with him, and give no heed to what he says, for he "is not of God." -C.H. Spurgeon

truth - 1 John 4

- ☐ Divide the lower part of your page into six sections. (If you'd like a lot of space to write, tape paper onto the edge of your page to make a hinge that flips open. When you make your lists, just flip it open and divide it into six parts!)

- ☐ Title the columns: truth about me, truth about others, truth about love, truth about abiding, truth about God, and truth about Jesus.

- ☐ First, truth about you. Read through the following verses and write down all the truth you find about you: verses 4, 6, 15, 17, 19-21. Write these as a statement of fact in first person. For example: I am from God. I have overcome.

- ☐ The second list is about others. Read verses 2, 3, 6, and 20-21. Write what you learn about others in question form because these are great questions to ask yourself about others and any teaching you hear. For example: Do they say Jesus was fully man (verse 2)?

- ☐ The third list is about love. Read the verses and write out the truth you find about love from verses 7-11 and 18-19. Read through your list and summarize it into 4 or 5 bullet points. Ask and answer: What does this teach me about God? How can I praise Him for this? What do I need to confess?

- ☐ Fourth, make a list about abiding by noting truths from verses 12-17. After you've made your notes, look up and write out the definition for abide. A regular dictionary or Bible dictionary works great. Rewrite a summary or a verse or two plugging in your definition for abide in place of the word. What does this teach you about God and your relationship with Him?

- ☐ Our next list is about God. Read through verses 7-8, 12 and 15-16, making notes of all the truths you learn about God. I love the commentary the ESV Study Bible gives for verse 8: "... 'God is love' means that God continually gives of Himself to others and seeks their benefit."

- ☐ The final list is all about Jesus. List what you learn about Him from verses 2, and 14-15. What do these teach you about Jesus? What do these last two columns on God and Jesus teach you about you?

- ☐ Look back over column one. Do you believe these truths about yourself? Why or why not? What can you do to make these truths more a part of your life?

truth - 1 John 5

☐ On a new page, title the top with ASSURANCE and tape or color the side of the page green, with TRUTH written out on the top outer corner of the page.

☐ Read through 1 John 5.

☐ God (and John) want believers to be assured. We have to replace the doubts and lies of the evil one with crucial truths. If we never get to the point of resting fully in Jesus and His righteousness given to us, Satan will multiply our doubt, uncertainty, and fear, rendering us useless in God's Kingdom. Satan loves to knock us down, get us to question our beliefs, and misunderstand (or not even know) what we believe. But God wants us to KNOW.

☐ In your journal make a list of all God says about you in this chapter. (Draw a piece of paper around it.) For example, I read 5:1 and wrote out: born of God. 5:2 says I love others, I love God, and I am unburdened by His commandments. Keep reading through the chapter and add to your list.

☐ Read John 14:1-7 and John 14:18-21. Summarize the main points in your journal. What truth does Jesus tell us in these verses? How does this matter in your life today?

☐ Read John 8:1-11 and draw a stone or rock. Jesus was the only one who had the right to throw the first stone. He alone was sinless. But He was the only one who **didn't want to**. Write out verse 11. You will have no peace and no true assurance until you rest in the fact that it's all about HIM. His payment for your sins on the cross. His righteousness given to you. It has nothing to do with what you do, everything to do with what He did.

☐ Write "confidence" in a big banner on your page. God wants us to live in confidence! It would be fun to draw a simple stick figure girl holding the banner. What should we have confidence in? Read verses 1-5, stopping after each sentence and writing what you can have confidence in, or what truth is stated. Do the same for verses 11-15, and 18-20.

pause and reflect

We are finished with our look at the truths in 1 John, but before we move on, turn to a new page in your journal and review all you learned.

- What stood out to you the most?
- What can you thank God for?
- What do these truths teach you about God?
- About yourself?
- Turn these truths into a prayer of thanksgiving and praise.

just & justifier

We *love* because He first loved us.

love - 1 John 1

- ☐ Take a moment before we start this new section to pray and ask for clarity and focus.

- ☐ Read chapter 1.

- ☐ Set up a new page, by titling the top with ASSURANCE. This time we're going to use pink for the side of each of these pages on love. Write LOVE on the top outer corner of the page.

- ☐ Draw a banner and write out the word love. The International Study Bible Encyclopedia defines love as: an earnest and anxious desire for and an active and beneficent interest in the well being of the one loved. In 1 John when we see the English word love, it is usually one of two different Greek words: *agapaō* or *agapē*. In chapter one we won't see either word, but we do see the results of it. Look up the definition of love and write it on your page.

- ☐ In your journal, draw a small group of bowling pin people. Near them write out (nice and big) the Greek word *agapaō* (love). What is the result of this love that affects other people in our life according to verse 7? Write your answer near your doodle.

- ☐ Now draw a simple cross and the Greek word *agapē*. This is the word for the highest most perfect kind of love, God's love. What is the result of God's love toward us (verses 1-5).

- ☐ Write out the definition of fellowship in your own words. The Greek word for fellowship is *koinonia*. Write that out nice and big. Thayer's Greek Lexicon says that *koinonia* is joint participation, partakers of the same mind of God and Christ. A relationship of shared resources and a shared life. Think of this in terms of both our relationship with other believers and our relationship with God. SHARED. We don't **add** Jesus to our life, we share in His life. We don't add relationships with other believers, we **share** life.

- ☐ How is your fellowship with God? Is it fear-based? Close? Intimate? Or is it more like a convenient (or inconvenient) distant relationship? How should your fellowship with God be if it was true *koinonia* or shared life with Him? Would it look any different? How?

love – 1 John 2

☐ Read chapter 2 and mark and label your page with "assurance" and "love."

☐ Draw a stone tablet or scroll and write out Leviticus 19:18 and Deuteronomy 6:5. Why did John focus on these two verses when he spoke of the old/new commandment when there are hundreds of other commandments that he could have referred to? He'll tell us in 3:11 (skip there now and peek).

☐ Look up Jesus' most important commands in Matthew 22:35-40 and John 13:34. (It would be fun to doodle Jesus speaking these words.) This old/new commandment is nothing the believers of his time (and ours) haven't heard before, but John knows it is important to remind and refresh the believer's hearts. Write out the verses or summarize in your journal.

☐ After reminding us of the new/old commandment, John writes the only command in this chapter: "Do not love this world or the things of this world." Write this command out in your journal, on a stone or scroll or next to a feather pen.

☐ Augustine, an early church father used a great illustration of God's love as the only love to be rooted and grounded in (Ephesians 3:17), and if we are not rooted in God's love, we'll be like a seedling trying to grow but strangled out by worldly love. *"How shall [love] be rooted there, amid the overgrown wilderness of the love of the world? Make clear riddance of the woods. A mighty seed you are about to put in: let there not be [anything] in the field which shall choke the seed. These are the uprooting words which He has said: 'Love not the world, neither the things that are in the world...'"*

☐ It would be memorable to draw a tiny seedling (rooted or growing out of the words "God's love") surrounded by big weeds and trees.

love - 1 John 2

- ☐ John isn't saying not to love the things that God has made, but he's warning against loving them more than the God who made them. (Romans 1:25) Augustine again makes a great illustration of a bride loving the ring more than her groom, figuring it is enough to have the ring and not need the groom or the marriage, or the love, or the companionship the ring represents. God's creation is His picture book of love to us. We can see His marks on everything and enjoy all His creation (1 Tim 6:17) but we must keep our love directed to the One who made it, not what was made. Don't love the ring more than the groom. (Another great doodle idea would be to draw a sparkling wedding ring and write out the bride illustration.)

- ☐ How can we tell if we are loving the world? John gives us three things to watch out for. Read verse 16 and write out the three things.

- ☐ What do those things look like in our modern lives? It will vary for each of us of course, but it is usually slow and unnoticed as it sneaks into life, leaving smudges and smears on a believer's heart. Write out any of these that might ring true for you in your journal... Do you find yourself demanding luxury because you deserve it? Or maybe you are buried in debt to the point that you can't sleep at night. Or you might be a little (or a lot) discontent with your life, your job, your house, your family. Or maybe it shows up in your giving... is it easier to spend on pleasing yourself than giving to God's work? Or maybe reading the Bible and praying may no longer stir your spirit but seem dry, boring, and not worth the effort. Is love of the world showing up in your life as you pull away from church, Bible study, or fellowship with other believers because you just don't enjoy it? (Remember from earlier, fellowship is shared life. Sharing takes time and effort and will rarely be instantaneous.)

- ☐ If any of these hit close to home, don't leave this section without checking your heart and bringing it before God.

- ☐ Is there anything else in your life that might be a sign of love of the world? Write it all down and bring it to God.

love – 1 John 3

- ☐ Read chapter 3 and label your page with "assurance" and "love."

- ☐ Look back on your notes from chapter three on truth. Remember that we are to behold God's love. We are to discern His love. Understand His love. Be amazed by His love. We are to experience His love and especially be skilled in His love. In your journal write out some of those definitions, or look up the word behold on blueletterBible.com and add any definitions that are meaningful.

behold

- ☐ How do we become skilled in His love so we understand and experience it as we should? By practice. If we practice God's kind of love (full, unconditional, steadfast, enduring, merciful) we'll become more and more skilled in how to love as Jesus loved. Take a few minutes and brainstorm how you can better discern, experience, and become skilled in His love. Write it all out. Then pray for insight for how you can put this into practice with the people in your life. Get as specific as possible.

- ☐ Has His love made a difference in your life? How so? Take a few minutes to write out how God's love has changed you. (This is an EXCELLENT start to writing out your testimony!)

- ☐ Highlight or underline every occurrence of the word love in this chapter. Make a list of all you find out about love. You might want to doodle a scrap of paper and make your list on that.

- ☐ Notice that salvation begins with love. Salvation isn't solely to get us into heaven. If that were the case, God could take us up to be with Him the instant we believed. The gospel redeems, but it also re-forms. Not just reform (as in a change of thought or behavior) but radically re-forms and completely changes our heart into a new form—one that the Holy Spirit can take up residence in. He could never live in our sin-filled heart; a heart transplant had to take place and a result of that is that we love differently than the world.

- ☐ Because of this heart transplant, you SHOULD feel differently when you are with others who have not been changed by the love of God. Have there been times that you have felt awkward or uncomfortable around unbelievers? (If not, why?) Jot some notes in your journal if you can think of examples.

love - 1 John 3

- ☐ The truth is that love for the brothers (3:14) and one another (3:11, 23) doesn't start with knuckling down and just doing it. It's not "today I will love that person that irritates me and has for years," but instead focusing your love on the One who first loved us . Then through abiding (resting, remaining, adhering or connecting to) in Him we are able to love as He loves.

- ☐ In reading verse 15 please remember that just because you don't enjoy being around another believer doesn't automatically mean you hate them. Loving isn't always going to be easy. In Mere Christianity, C.S. Lewis says loving those who are hard to love means feeling about them as we do about ourselves. Honestly, there are times I'm not fond of myself, but I still pray that God will change me and grow inside me. Abiding in His love (2:24-28; 3:6), hoping in Him (3:3), purifying yourself (3:3) and practicing righteousness (3:7) result in love. It's not knuckling down and forcing yourself to love, it's losing yourself in Christ and being transformed into His image that re-forms your heart and grows His love there.

- ☐ So how do you develop that love and passion for God? Brainstorm a list of things you know you could do today or this week to develop your passion toward God. Then honestly think through what you cut out of your busy days and weeks to make more time to get to know and love Him more.

- ☐ In your journal, make a list of the four points above that grow our love (abiding, hoping, purifying, and practicing). After each point, look up the verse referenced and write it out.

- ☐ Write out what you can do to grow in each area. Be specific with the details: What will you do? What will you cut out of your day to make more room for this? How can you pray specifically for this?

abide

hope

purify

practice

love – 1 John 4

☐ Read chapter 4 and mark and label your page with "assurance" and "love."

☐ On your journal page, make two columns. At the top of the first column draw a big heart and inside it write 1 John 4:7-21. At the top of the second column draw another heart and inside it write John 15:9-17.

☐ Read through 1 John 4:7-21 again and write bullet points about love in the first column. Do the same for John 15:9-17. After you've made your lists, compare and contrast what you wrote down.

☐ Love is proof of God living in us and us abiding in Him. God's love is planted by the Sprit in our newly re-formed heart. Write out Galatians 5:22-23, and circle or draw a heart around the first fruit. Love doesn't have to be forced. Because the Spirit inside us, love is natural. But, because we live in a sinful world, and are sinful people, we will always battle selfish desires that war against love for God and others.

☐ In his book, A Loving Life, Paul Miller said: *"When you realize that death is at the center of love, it is quietly liberating. Instead of fighting the death that comes with love, you embrace what your Father has given you."* Did you get that? Death is at the center of love. Death! The death of Christ was the center of God's love for us, and death to ourselves is the center of God's love in us.

☐ Who are some people that you have a hard time loving? What part of YOU is getting in the way of loving them the way Christ loves us? Where do you need the Spirit to work in your heart to help soften these places? Take some time to pray and ask the Spirit to search your heart as only He can.

☐ The love of God is already in our hearts, we just have to remove enough of ourselves to let that love for others grow. I think of it as one of those silver scratch off tickets. Scratch off enough of that silver covering and you'll be able to experience what's underneath.

love – 1 John 4

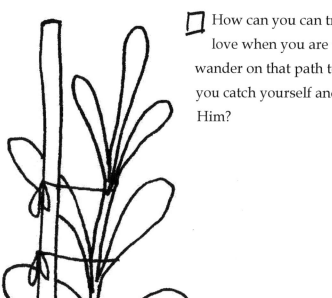

- ☐ Draw a young plant tied to a small, straight pole. Next to it draw some thistles and thorny plants.

- ☐ Near your plants, write out verse 16 (the second part) and Hebrews 3:12-13.

- ☐ Love is the normal output of the Christian life because it is the work of the Spirit in our hearts, but we must put it into practice. We must train our love (like training a plant to grow straight) by tying ourselves (or abiding) in the right thing. When we abide in hard feelings and bitterness it leads to a bitter, unbelieving and hardened heart. But we can choose to abide in Him, in love, and in God.

- ☐ How can you can train yourself to abide in His love when you are tempted to let your mind wander on that path toward bitterness? How will you catch yourself and direct it back to abiding in Him?

1 John 5
love

ASSURANCE

love - 1 John 5

☐ Read chapter 5 and mark and label your page with "assurance" and "love."

☐ In chapter 5, love is mentioned only in the first 3 verses, and they are intermingled with truth and obedience and a new item, faith.

☐ In your journal, toward the side of the page, draw a stick or bowling pin person to represent you. Next to "you" draw three arrows pointing away, one angled up, one straight, and one angled down. Draw a cross at the end of the angled up arrow, write the word GOD at the end of the straight arrow, and draw 3 or 4 stick figures after the angled down arrow.

☐ Near the arrow pointing toward the cross, write "believes," and near the arrow pointing to God, write "loves," and near the arrow pointing to the stick figures, write "loves."

☐ Between the cross, God, and people draw two way arrows going from them to each other and from them back to you. It's all tied together. If we believe in Jesus (not a mere affirmation of religion, but Jesus as our Savior and God) we have been born of God and love God and love others. It's automatic. It's all twined together. But when too much of our sinful self gets in the way, things start to unravel. What do you think? Write out your thoughts.

love - 1 John 5

- ☐ Now let's look at faith. This is the first and only time faith appears in this whole letter, so let's pay close attention. In your journal, draw a big shield with a cross on it and "faith" written under the cross.

- ☐ Above the cross, write "overcomer." If you've been born of God, you've already overcome the world according to verse 4. And you've overcome it by your faith in Christ.

- ☐ Look up John 16:33 and write it out near your shield. Do the same with 1 Corinthians 15:57 and Ephesians 6:16. We have overcome because Christ overcame and gave that victory to us.

- ☐ Read through John 16:33 again. This time, imagine Jesus talking directly to you. Telling you this truth, eye to eye. There is no doubt in this statement. He didn't say "if you try hard, do the right things, and don't mess up…" No, He simply wants us to have peace in the truth that He has already overcome. How can this give you peace? Journal your thoughts.

- ☐ This should wrap you up in assurance because even though none of us have loved others perfectly, we have been loved perfectly, and as long as we allow the Holy Spirit access to all the areas of our life, He will do His work in growing us more like Christ. How does this give you assurance?

assurance

"Follow on to know the Lord. Labor to know Him more clearly and more fully, to know more of Christ and to know Him to better purpose, so as to be more like Him and to love Him better."

—Matthew Henry

God is love - a guided meditation

The majority of this chapter is about love. John really wants us to get it.

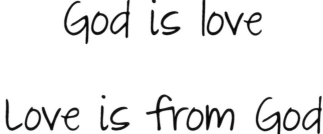

God is love

Love is from God

God so loved us

Love is perfected in us

For this section in love, let's meditate on the phrase "God is love." I'm going to help you work through it with a few Biblical meditation techniques, but there is a more complete guide in the back of this book. Biblical meditation is filling the mind with God and His truth, not emptying the mind like eastern meditation practices. (See Joshua 1:8, Psalm 63:6, and Psalm 77:6). We are to meditate and diligently search our heart, seeking out error and sin to work actively against it. Then we are to fill ourselves with truth from God's word so God's Spirit can put it to use in our lives.

☐ In your journal write out "God is Love" in the center of your page then write out verse 16.

☐ Now rewrite "**GOD** is love" and bold or highlight or color the word GOD. Say it to yourself with emphasis on GOD. Write out any notes, even a simple thought on how emphasizing the word God changes or highlights anything. Do the same method, but next emphasize **IS**. Finish by emphasizing **LOVE**. Adding any notes or insights. (Challenge: write out at least 5 observations for each emphasized word.)

☐ Next, write down what you notice about God's love (according to all we've studied about love so far in 1 John). Is there anything you wonder about God's love? Just brainstorm and write it all down.

God is love - a guided meditation

- ☐ Write out and answer: What effect does God's love have on me? On the world?

- ☐ What fruit does God's love create in me? The world?

- ☐ What characteristics, properties and attributes does God's love have? Look back on all your notes so far on love from 1 John.

- ☐ Look up cross-references or any other verses about His love that come to mind.

- ☐ Compare and contrast: What compares to or is similar to God's love? What contrasts with or is opposite of God's love?

- ☐ What are some titles or names of God's love? What have people in the Bible called God's love? What does God call it? (You might want to do a search on blueletterbible.org for LOVE in the Old Testament with some great descriptions like: unfailing, great, faithful, etc.)

- ☐ Now ask yourself: Have I fully grasped this?

- ☐ How would truly understanding this amazing love make me different?

pause and reflect

We are finished with our look at love in 1 John, but before we move on, turn to a new page in your journal and review all you learned.

- ☐ What stood out to you the most?
- ☐ What can you thank God for?
- ☐ What do these truths teach you about God?
- ☐ About yourself?
- ☐ Turn these thoughts into a prayer of thanksgiving and praise.

By this we know that we love the children of God, when we love God and **obey** His commandments.

Obedience – 1 John 1

- ☐ Set up a new page, by titling the top with ASSURANCE. This time we're going to use blue for the side of each of these pages on obedience. Write OBEDIENCE on the top outer corner of the page.

- ☐ Read chapter 1.

- ☐ Draw a banner or flag and write "obedience" inside it. Make a list of what you learn about obedience in verses 5-10 under your banner.

- ☐ Review your list. Notice there are no specific "don't do this" types of lists, but rather a general theme of fellowship, walking in the light, and confession of sin. What does this teach you about God?

- ☐ Draw a scroll, or John reading from a scroll. In verse 5 he says "This is the message…" What is that message? Near your doodle, or on your scroll write out the rest of verse 5.

- ☐ Notice the string of "if we's" John writes in verses 6 to 10. Write each "if we say" in a speech bubble, and the other "if we's" around them.

- ☐ What do these "if we's" teach you? What truths do they teach? What assurance do they give you? Write out your thoughts on your journal page.

Obedience is a very important part of why John is writing. Throughout his letter he urges us to grow in our understanding (truth) and to obey from a willing heart. Our walk MUST match our talk. As believers we have only two choices, we either walk in the light and have fellowship and cleansing from sin, or we walk in darkness, lie, and don't practice the truth. There is no gray area here. The Bible doesn't have a complete list of "do's and don'ts" for the believer. Anyone can follow a list of rules if they grit their teeth and try hard enough. And they can follow those rules with a heart that is still disobedient and rebellious. But God wants to capture our whole heart so that obedience naturally flows from that. Are you walking in the light? Are there areas of your life that you are still in darkness? Worse yet, are there areas in your life you are deliberately keeping in darkness? If you say they are not sin, but God says otherwise, John makes it very clear that you are calling God a liar. If you are making excuses for any habitual or hidden sin in your life, stop now and confess and ask for His forgiveness. Ask God to help make our talk match up with our walk.

Obedience – 1 John 1

- ☐ This life (and the Bible) is not a to-do checklist to gain salvation — salvation is only gained through accepting Christ's completed work on the cross as payment for your sin. He has already done it all. 2 Timothy 1:8-10 says: *"He saved us and called us not because of anything we have done, but because of His own purpose and grace which He gave us in Christ Jesus..."* With that in mind, what *should* obedience in your life look like? Does it look like that? How do you know when you are obeying out of fear or duty rather than love? Journal your thoughts.

- ☐ Our obedience is not to earn anything. So then, what is the point of obedience? Take some time to think through this and write our your thoughts.

- ☐ Obedience is to honor and glorify Him who obeyed perfectly for us and then gave that righteousness to us. Each time we say no to ourselves and yes to God, He grows us and changes us to be more like Christ. What is one area of your life that you feel God tugging you toward obedience in? How can you walk in the light in this area?

- ☐ Write out the quote below in your journal. What kind of people does God want? What is that "particular sort" of people He wants?

> "We might think that God wanted simply obedience to a set of rules; wheras He really wants people of a particular sort."
>
> —C.S. Lewis

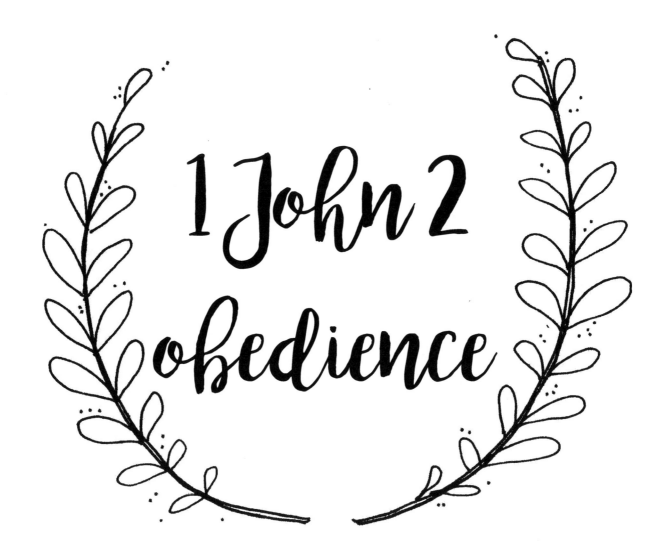

Obedience – 1 John 2

- [ ] Set up and mark your page with ASSURANCE and OBEDIENCE.

- [ ] Read chapter 2.

- [ ] Obedience is one of the tests John keeps returning to as a way for us check if we truly know Christ. If we know Him, we'll desire to obey and keep His commandments. According to the Blue Letter Bible Lexicon, the definition of the word "keep" is to attend to carefully, to take care of, to guard. Strong's definition also includes the idea of guarding by keeping the eye upon. Draw a padlock to symbolize something well kept, then write out verse three with one of the definitions substituted for the word "keep." (Or, for Extra Credit, write out the sentence multiple times, substituting all the different definitions.) Does it give you a different perspective? How should this affect you? Why does this matter in your life today?

- [ ] Do you hate sin? Do you hate the pollution of sin in your heart? Or do you hate only the consequences or trouble that sin causes? Hating only the result or only the pain sin causes will leave you with little to no peace in your life. Sin tempts you, tantalizes you, promises you happiness, entertainment, and enjoyment. Then when you succumb, it entangles you and tightens the cords mercilessly. Sin is a lying, cheating, deceitful jerk. Have you experienced this in your life? Write out a few examples of how it ended up stinging you.

- [ ] Read through the quote on the next page.

- [ ] Draw an open and closed padlock and write your thoughts to the following questions under each. How well do you know your own weaknesses that lead to sin? Do you know when, or in what situations, you are more likely to succumb to sin? When is your padlock opened and your heart unguarded? When is it locked and you are at your strongest?

"Many men live in the dark to themselves all their days; whatever else they know, they know not themselves. They know their outward estates, how rich they are, and the condition of their bodies as to health and sickness they are careful to examine; but as to their inward man, and their principles as to God and eternity, they know little or nothing of themselves. Indeed, few labor to grow wise in this matter, few study themselves as they ought, are acquainted with the evils of their own hearts as they ought; on which yet the whole course of their obedience... does depend."
- John Owen

Obedience - 1 John 2

- Again, the main theme of 1 John is assurance, and if you're feeling conviction here, take it as part of the assurance that you are a believer. In <u>Mere Christianity</u>, C.S. Lewis says *"When a man is getting better he understands more and more clearly the evil that is still left in him. When a man is getting worse, he understands his own badness less and less. A moderately bad man knows he is not very good; a thoroughly bad man thinks he is all right."*

- In this life we are supposed to be continually progressing in our knowledge of the truth, love for God and others, and obedience to Christ. That makes us more and more like Him and prepares us for our forever home with Him. Use any conviction to sharpen you and make you more aware of sin and the need for obedience in your life.

"How can we love Christ and neglect duty to Christ?"
-Isaac Ambrose

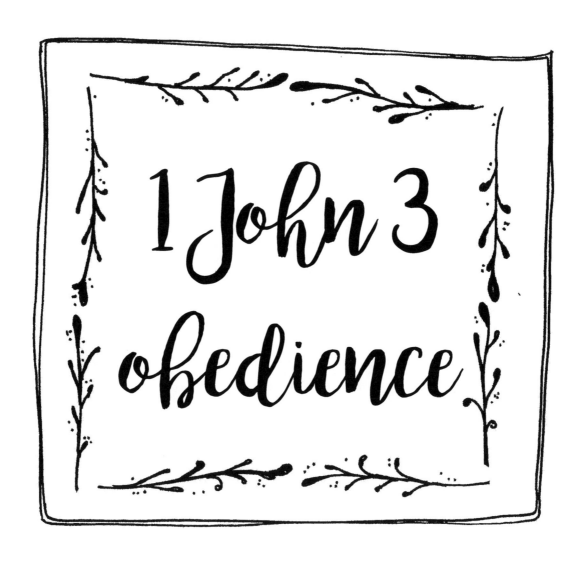

Obedience – 1 John 3

- ☐ Set up and mark your page with ASSURANCE and OBEDIENCE.

- ☐ Read chapter 3.

- ☐ What are we to do based on our position as adopted children of God? Read verses 3-7 and write out what you find. Also look up and write out: Romans 13:14, 2 Corinthians 7:1, 2 Peter 2:11, Galatians 5:24 and James 4:1-3. What does this teach you about God? About yourself?

- ☐ Draw a cleaning solution bottle or bleach jug. Next to those write out: how do we purify ourselves? Look up and write out Romans 13:14. To "put on" means to sink into, clothe yourself, envelop in, hide in. As Matthew Henry puts it, it is *"...to become so possessed of the mind of Christ as in thought, feeling, and action to resemble Him and as it were, reproduce the life He lived."* What, specifically, would this look like in your life today? This week? This month? This year?

- ☐ In verse 4 John gives us the definition of sin. (Remember when we saw this in the section on truth?) Write out verse 4 and draw the word sin, big and scribbly and black. Now write out your own definition of sin—referring back to this verse.

- ☐ In verses 4, 6, 8, and 9 John makes it clear that a Christian should not be living, abiding, and practicing sin. In these verses he does not refute the truth in verses 1:10 and 2:1. He is not saying we won't sin or that we can become sinless in this life, but he is saying that we will not have a lifestyle marked by sin. Draw a heart with a seedling in it. Our heart has been re-formed, we've had a radical heart transplant and now God's seed lives and grows there. Look up and write out 1 Peter 1:22-23 next to it. What difference should this make in your life today?

Obedience - 1 John 3

☐ In your journal, draw some stairs with a stick person going up them, or just an arrow pointing up the stairs. At the top of the stairs draw clouds to represent heaven and at the bottom a world or the word "sin." In our lives here on earth we will never reach perfection (1 John 1:8,10). We will never get to a point where we don't sin. But because our hearts are changed, we don't HAVE to sin. We are no longer under the control of this world. We have the power of the Holy Spirit living in us to help us grow in truth and to convict us. God expects us to always be moving up those stairs and growing more like Christ (progressive sanctification.) But really, in life these stairs are  more like a downward moving escalator. Because we live in a sin-filled world, the escalator is always moving downward. If you are not actively climbing toward God, you're moving downward toward sin. What is the next step you need to take upward? What do you need to give up? How do you need to sacrifice? (Psalm 4:5)

☐ The Spirit will convict, but there is always the scary truth that a Christian can be hardened by sin and God will give them over to sin that is habitually practiced (Hebrews 3:13). We should never be at peace with sin. Are there any sins you are at peace with in your life  right now? Has the battle been long and wearisome and it's easier to just justify the sin? Do you wonder if it's worth the hassle of fighting? Are you are harboring a pet sin because it feels good (in the moment) or is just too overwhelming to think of how to battle it? Has bitterness been sheltered and overgrown in your heart? Write out your thoughts and then journal and take them to God.

Do you mortify; do you make it your daily work; be always at it while you live; cease not a day from this work; be killing sin or it will be killing you.
-John Owen

Obedience – 1 John 4

☐ Draw a stone tablet and on it write out 1 John 2:7. This is the new/old commandment that John says is imperative to obey. Since God is love, we too should be distinctly marked by love. Yes, in this sinful world we will never be able to fully, unselfishly love others because we're always wanting or needing something in return for our love. But we have the perfect example in Christ. In his book, King's Cross, Tim Keller puts it this way:

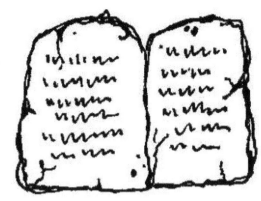

"What we need is someone to love us who doesn't need us at all. Someone who loves us radically, unconditionally, vulnerably. Someone who loves us just for our sake. If we received that kind of love, that would so assure us of our value, it would so fill us up, that maybe we could start to give love like that too. Who can give love with no need? Jesus."

☐ In this chapter, John beautifully marries all the themes of truth, obedience, and love together in a few sentences. Write out verses 7, 10-11, and 21. Look up and write out Galatians 6:2 also or any other cross references you find. What do these verses teach you about truth, love, and obedience?

☐ So again, in all areas (truth, obedience, and love), we need to be moving up the escalator in obedience to Him. It is not perfection He is looking for, it is a heart that is growing more and more like His. He wants us to keep taking those steps up the escalator to Him. Write a note to yourself to remember "Growth, not perfection." How do these verses give you assurance?

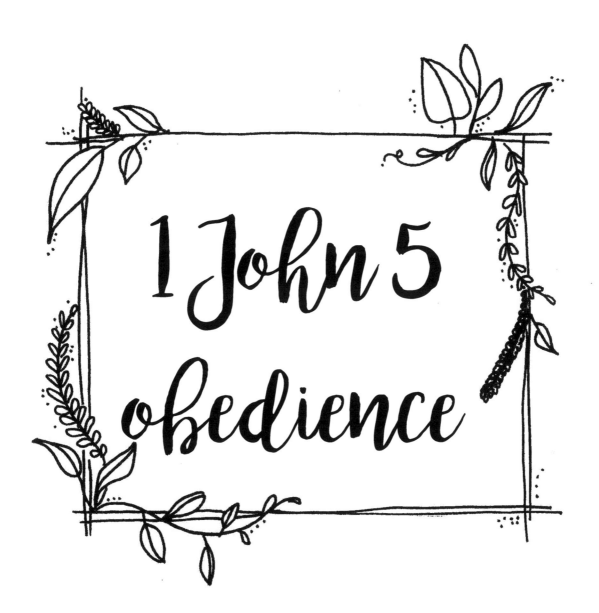

Obedience – 1 John 5

28

- ☐ Set up and mark your page with ASSURANCE and OBEDIENCE.

- ☐ Read chapter 5.

- ☐ Does God really want us to be assured of our position in Christ? Twenty eight times in this book John uses the word "know." Write "know" really big in your journal and then write a big block letter "28 times" in your journal. Yes, God really, really wants us to get this. It's time we stop crippling ourselves with questions and doubts. This is the book of ASSURANCE. How has this epistle given you assurance? Have you doubted your faith in the past? If so, after working through the book of 1 John, has that changed?

know

- ☐ Flip back through your journal and review all your work so far. (I'd love to see what you've learned, I'll bet it's beautiful!) Write what stood out to you that you feel God wants you to KNOW. Get specific. You could even make separate lists of what He wants you to know about Him, His Son, your walk, your love, and your obedience.

- ☐ In your journal in big bold letters write TRUTH – LOVE – OBEDIENCE. Draw an arrow from truth pointing to love, and from love pointing to obedience.

- ☐ This study was written in a specific order. We should know TRUTH about God and what He says and from that we fall more and more in LOVE with Him. Just like all relationships, the more we know about the person the more we love them. Knowing truth about God leads to loving Him more and obedience automatically follows. It's not the other way around. We never obey to earn anything (good standing with God, salvation, or anything else). That is fear based obedience. (We fear we won't get what we need or want, or we fear that we'll lose what we have.) A Bible commentator said that young children often obey out of fear (of punishment). As they age, they begin to obey because the commands and requests make sense. But what a delight it is to parent a child who obeys out of love! 1 John was written to show us that God wants to capture our heart. We obey because we have been given so much!

truth → love → obedience

Obedience – 1 John 5

☐ Draw a Bible and near it write out verse 3 and 4.

☐ Look up John 14:15 and Matthew 11:29-30. One Bible commentator stated that Jesus (and John) are not just talking about the Ten Commandments, but all the commandments given in the Bible, even the hard ones in the New Testament (like love one another). This does not it will be *easy*, but for a believer it should not be a *burden* to obey God's commands.

"If [John] wished us to know that we have eternal life, brothers and sisters, let us try to know it… are you not bidden to make your calling and election sure? Are you not a thousand times over exhorted to rejoice in the Lord and to give thanks continually? But how can you rejoice if the dark suspicion haunts you, that perhaps, after all, you have not the life of God? You must get this question settled, or you cannot rest in the Lord and wait patiently for Him." -C.H. Spurgeon

☐ Read verses 13-21 again. Flip back in your journal to the "we know" page you've been working on. Salvation is 100% completely God's work and you will have no peace, no assurance or confidence until you realize that it's all God. It's not anything you have done or will do. Salvation is God's work and God's righteousness given to you, and His payment on your behalf. How does this give you assurance?

☐ Assurance, however is on us. THAT is our work. Assurance will never come to the lazy, distracted, or too busy. Assurance requires being diligent. Working to find out truth. Practicing love and obedience and putting faith to work (James 2:18-28). I love this quote by Puritan Pastor John Flavel: *"God does not usually indulge negligent souls with the comforts of assurance; He will not so much as seem to patronize sloth and carelessness. He will give assurance, but it shall be in His own way… Those are mistaken who think that assurance may be obtained without labor."*

☐ So what are you doing? What's your plan? Write out what you are currently doing to grow in your faith and knowledge of God.

Obedience - 1 John 5

☐ Now brainstorm some other things you could do to grow more. Write down lots and lots of ideas, not just the ones you think you have time for. Keep brainstorming until you have nothing left.

☐ After you've made your list, look it over and choose just one thing you'd like to work on right now. Then, decide what you need to cut from your day so you have the time to do it.

☐ The very last sentence in this book is powerful. "Little children, keep yourselves from idols." John Calvin once said that our heart is a factory of idols. When we think we've overcome one, another comes out of the forge, fresh and shiny. Have you seen this in your life?

☐ The definition of keep is to guard, to protect, to preserve safe and unimpaired. It's from a root word that means isolation. Given those definitions, how can you keep yourself from idols? Write out specific ideas and pray for the Lord to reveal any current idols your factory might have already churned out.

"The use of doctrine is not only to initiate the ignorant in the knowledge of Christ, but also to confirm those more and more who have been already taught."

–John Calvin

pause and reflect

We are finished with our look at obedience in 1 John, but before we move on, turn to a new page in your journal and review all you learned.

- What stood out to you the most?
- What can you thank God for?
- What do these truths teach you about God?
- About yourself?
- Turn these thoughts into a prayer of thanksgiving and praise.

1 John conclusion

ASSURANCE

conclusion – 1 John

Wow! What an incredible ride we've been on! I pray you got as much out of working through this study as I did in preparing it for you!

If you're not quite ready to end your time in 1 John yet, here are some other ideas:

- ☐ I encourage you not to put this away and think of it as "done," but to spend a couple of days or a week reviewing all you've learned. Go through your journal and add some more doodles, notes, highlights, or fill in anything you might have missed.

- ☐ Turn your thoughts and notes in each chapter into a prayer to thank God and write out specific requests from each of the chapters.

- ☐ Read through John chapters 14-17 and note all the similarities from those chapters and 1 John.

- ☐ Make separate meditation pages for key verses that stand out to you.

Thank you so much for supporting Journal and Doodle Bible Studies! Your support makes it possible for me to keep writing and doodling. It is my greatest desire that these studies will encourage, strengthen, and spur you on to keep advancing the kingdom of God. Before I go, I have to give a big thank you to the friends who kept encouraging me to keep persevering, especially Kerry, Kristen, Kira, and Mackenzie. You guys probably will never know how instrumental you were to keeping this study alive! THANK YOU! Most of all, though, all praise and glory goes to my Savior, Jesus Christ. Not to me, Lord, not to me, but to Your name be the glory.

Kari

Some more Puritan goodness for you. You're welcome.

Signs of living to please God
Richard Baxter

See therefore that you live upon God's approval as that which you chiefly seek, and will suffice you: which you may discover by these signs.

1. You will be most careful to understand the Scripture, to know what doth please and displease God.

2. You will be more careful in the doing of every duty, to fit it to the pleasing of God than men.

3. You will look to your hearts, and not only to your actions; to your ends, and thoughts, and the inward manner and degree.

4. You will look to secret duties as well as public and to that which men see not, as well as unto that which they see.

5. You will reverence your consciences, and have much to do with them, and will not slight them: when they tell you of God's displeasure, it will disquiet you; when they tell you of his approval, it will comfort you.

6. Your pleasing men will be charitable for their good, and pious in order to the pleasing of God, and not proud and ambitious for your honour with them, nor impious against the pleasing of God.

7. Whether men be pleased or displeased, or how they judge of you, or what they call you, will seem a small matter to you, as their own interest, in comparison to God's judgment. You live not on them. You can bear their displeasure, censures, and reproaches, if God be but pleased. These will be your evidences.

📔 In your journal, rewrite each of these points in your own words, applying them to your life in light of what you've learned from 1 John.

Meditation Guide

What is the main idea or theme of the verse or verses? (Sum it up in a simple phrase or single word.)

In context of your word or phrase, answer these questions:

- What causes it?
- Where do you see it (or not see it) in the world? In your life?
- What does deliberate use of it look like? Casual use? Neglect of it?
- What effect does it have? What fruit does it create?
- What characteristics, properties, and/or attributes does it have?
- What contrasts with or is opposite of it? What compares to or is similar to it?
- What are its titles and names? What do people call it? What does God call it?
- Look up any cross reference or similar verses and write or summarize them.
- What are some specific stories in life or scripture of this put into action?
- What have you believed or disbelieved about this?
- What does this teach you about God?
- What applications can you make from this? What should you do or stop doing in light of this?
- How should this truth change you?

Prayer Guide

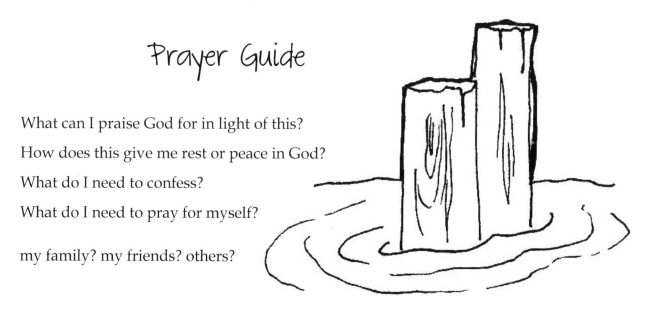

What can I praise God for in light of this?

How does this give me rest or peace in God?

What do I need to confess?

What do I need to pray for myself?

my family? my friends? others?

Find all the Journal and Doodle Bible studies on my website
www.StoneSoupforFive.com

©Kari Denker 2017

Made in United States
Orlando, FL
28 December 2023